My Beautiful Present

Written by
BRITTANY PUTHUKERIL

Illustrated by
SAMANTHA MATHEW

WestBow Press books may be ordered through booksellers or by contacting:

WestBow Press
A Division of Thomas Nelson & Zondervan
1663 Liberty Drive
Bloomington, IN 47403
www.westbowpress.com
844-714-3454

Because of the dynamic nature of the Internet, any web addresses or links contained in this book may have changed since publication and may no longer be valid. The views expressed in this work are solely those of the author and do not necessarily reflect the views of the publisher, and the publisher hereby disclaims any responsibility for them.

Any people depicted in stock imagery provided by Getty Images are models, and such images are being used for illustrative purposes only.
Certain stock imagery © Getty Images.

Interior Image Credit: Samantha Mathew

Scriptures taken from the Holy Bible, New International Version®, NIV®. Copyright © 1973, 1978, 1984, 2011 by Biblica, Inc.™ Used by permission of Zondervan. All rights reserved worldwide. www.zondervan.com The "NIV" and "New International Version" are trademarks registered in the United States Patent and Trademark Office by Biblica, Inc.™ All rights reserved.

ISBN: 979-8-3850-2457-5 (sc)
ISBN: 979-8-3850-2458-2 (e)

Library of Congress Control Number: 2024908521

Print information available on the last page.

WestBow Press rev. date: 05/03/2024

WestBow
P R E S S®
A DIVISION OF THOMAS NELSON
& ZONDERVAN

To my beautiful boys, Jace and Jordan,
who arrived right on time

To my sweet husband, Ben,
who supports all my dreams and gave me the
courage to share my story with others

To my loving mom, Lovely,
who prays daily for her children and
for being my best friend

When I was a young girl, I prayed for you.
I dreamed of being a mom.
I didn't know the journey ahead would be difficult.

But my God already knew that at the right time,
You would be my beautiful present.

I wait with excitement,
Dreaming of names and treasures,
Feeling a glimmer of hope.
It is the hope of having you,
The hope of creating memories.

My God knows at the right time,
You will be my beautiful present.

Suddenly,
Hope turns into doubt.
The difficult journey begins.
My heart is feeling sad.
My strength is wearing thin.
I fear my dream will never happen.

Will God give me my beautiful present?

Time passes, and I wish my present would come sooner.
My gift isn't ready yet, and I am growing impatient.
"Why, God? Why?"

Will I ever get to hold you?
My heart is not ready to surrender.

But my God knows that at the right time,
You will be my beautiful present.

There is a fighting spirit within me.
I will not be discouraged.
My heart softens and starts to
give in to God's great plan.
My hope lives in the one who cares for me.
God cares for me.

He already knows that at the right time,
You will be my beautiful present.

Sometimes I don't understand the journey.
Some days are harder than others.
But after years of waiting, I still have hope.
I've got a promise I can hold on to in the middle of the struggle.

You hold my future, God.
You already know that at the right time,
My beautiful present will arrive.

One day a sweet peace fills my heart.
Something special is growing inside my belly.
My beautiful present is here.
And it is the right time, His perfect time.

I never gave up, even when things looked
hopeless. It was a hard journey
But one that I would do all over again—
Because it gave me you.

My beautiful baby, you are my precious gift.
You are my dream come true,
God's special child.
You are so loved.

Thank you, God, for my beautiful present.

"Now to Him who is able to do immeasureably more than all we ask or imagine, according to His power that is at work within us, to Him be glory in the church and in Christ Jesus throughout all generations, forever and ever! Amen."

Ephesians 3: 20-21

Note from the Author

I wrote this children's book for my children, Jace and Jordan, because I want them to know how precious their story is. It's difficult to explain concepts such as infertility, miscarriage, and deferred hope to children, but it's important for them to understand that sometimes God puts those dreams on hold while He prepares something even better for us.

We each have our own journey—journeys of loss and hope. It's hard to wait for something you desire, and it's even harder to hear a no or a not yet from God. But He knows our lives better than anyone. God created us beautiful in His image. We are worthy and strong enough to endure the hard things because of God and because of the Gospel.

Maybe you're still waiting on your present, or perhaps it's not in God's perfect plan for you. Regardless of the situation you're facing, know that the greatest present already given is that of salvation. You can have that at any moment.

This journey is not over yet; don't miss out on God's abundant blessings. Give your heart to Jesus today.

This is my greatest mission: to love God with all my heart, to share about His free gift, and to serve others with unconditional love.

Jace and Jordan, my prayer is that this would be your greatest mission as well, because your lives gave God glory! This is your beautiful story, and I thank God for it every day.

Printed in the United States
by Baker & Taylor Publisher Services